Martial Arts

Karate
Strikes

by Stuart Schwartz
and Craig Conley

Consultant:
Mark Willie, Instructor
Central Minnesota Karate
Mankato State University

CAPSTONE
HIGH/LOW BOOKS
an imprint of Capstone Press
Mankato, Minnesota

Capstone High/Low Books are published by Capstone Press
818 North Willow Street • Mankato, MN 56001
http://www.capstone-press.com

Library of Congress Cataloging-in-Publication Data
Schwartz, Stuart, 1945–
Karate strikes/by Stuart Schwartz and Craig Conley.
p. cm.—(Martial arts)
Includes bibliographical references (p. 45) and index.
Summary: A general description of karate, including its origins and
development, warm-up exercises, basic and advanced strikes, and safety
aspects.
ISBN 0-7368-0010-7
1. Karate—Juvenile literature. [1. Karate.] I. Conley, Craig, 1965– . II. Title.
III. Series: Martial arts (Mankato, Minn.)
GV1114.3.S36   1999
796.815—dc21
                                                        98-18637
                                                          CIP
                                                          AC

Editorial Credits
Cara Van Voorst, editor; James Franklin, cover designer and illustrator;
  Sheri Gosewisch, photo researcher

Photo Credits
All photographs by Gallery 19/Gregg R. Andersen.

Table of Contents

Chapter 1

Practicing Karate

Karate is a Japanese word that means empty hand. Karate students learn to defend themselves. They use their hands and feet as weapons to defend themselves. Students of karate are called karate-ka. Karate-ka learn blocks, kicks, strikes, and punches.

Most people can practice karate. But people should check with doctors before they start karate training. The doctors make sure the people are healthy enough for karate training.

Where Karate Started
People on Okinawa Island near Japan developed karate in the 1600s. Karate is a martial art. A martial art is a style of self-defense or fighting. Many martial arts

Karate students learn to defend themselves with their hands and feet.

Some karate-ka practice outside.

come from Asia. People in different areas of
Okinawa and Japan developed their own styles
of karate. The movements described in this
book are Shotokan style.

Gichin Funakoshi taught the Shotokan style
of karate on Okinawa Island in the early 1900s.
The Emperor of Japan asked Funakoshi to
demonstrate the Shotokan style of karate at his
palace. The emperor liked the Shotokan-style

movements Funakoshi performed. The emperor asked Funakoshi to open a karate school. Funakoshi taught Shotokan karate to Japanese people until his death in 1957. People in Okinawa and Japan first used karate to defend themselves. They later also practiced karate as a sport.

North Americans first learned karate from a Japanese sensei (SEN-say) named Oshima. Sensei means teacher in Japanese. Karate schools throughout the United States teach Shotokan karate today.

Many karate-ka train for karate competitions. A competition is a contest of skill. People around the world now learn karate for self-defense and for sport.

Places to Practice

Karate-ka can practice karate in any open space. Some karate-ka practice outside or in large rooms at their homes. Other karate-ka practice in dojos. A dojo is a karate school.

A dojo has a wide, open room. Karate-ka practice basic karate movements in this room.

There are usually mirrors on the walls of dojo rooms. Karate-ka look in the mirrors to see if they are performing moves correctly. They can move their bodies to correct positions while looking in the mirrors.

Karate Strikes

Karate strikes are attacking movements. Karate-ka use their arms to strike. The elbow is the center of movement in a strike. A strike is a snapping movement of the forearm from the elbow. The elbow and shoulder should stay relaxed during a strike until the moment of impact.

The karate-ka's hand can be either open or closed during a strike. Sometimes a karate-ka uses different hand positions to strike. Open-hand positions and fists are common hand positions.

Karate strikes are attacking movements.

Chapter 2

Stretching Exercises

Karate-ka warm up before workouts to help prevent injuries. Karate-ka might injure muscles and joints if they do not warm up.

Any loose-fitting clothing works well for karate practice. Most karate-ka practice in gi (GEE). A gi is a loose-fitting, cotton uniform. Karate-ka tie their gi with belts. Different colored belts represent the skill levels of the students. Beginning karate-ka wear white belts. The most advanced students wear black belts.

A karate-ka stretches her arms and upper body before practicing strikes. Neck rotations, arm rotations, upper body rotations, and body stretches relax the body before striking.

Most karate-ka wear gi when they practice.

A rotation is a circular movement. Karate-ka do each stretch about five times.

Neck Rotations and Arm Rotations

A karate-ka tips her head to the right to begin a neck rotation. She then rolls it to the front and to the left in a circular motion. The student rolls her head from the left to the back and to the right. This completes a full circle neck rotation. She then rolls her head the other way.

Arm rotations help loosen shoulder and arm muscles. A karate-ka begins an arm rotation by standing with her feet shoulder width apart and her arms at her sides. She then swings one arm up and backward in a circle. The karate-ka repeats the movement with her other arm.

Upper Body Rotations and Body Stretches

Upper body rotations help stretch stomach and back muscles. The karate-ka stands with her feet shoulder width apart and her hands on her hips. Then she slowly rotates her upper body

Upper body rotations stretch stomach muscles.

to the right. Then she rotates her upper body to her left side.

A karate-ka stands with her hands on her hips to begin a body stretch. Her feet are shoulder width apart. She clasps her hands above her head and stretches her arms upward as far as she can. The karate-ka bends to each side from her waist.

A karate-ka bends to each side from her waist during a body stretch.

Chapter 3

Basic Strikes

Beginning karate-ka learn basic strikes. These include the back-fist strike, the hammer-fist strike, and the knife-hand strike. Strikes are quick movements. A karate-ka snaps her elbow and quickly withdraws her forearm during a strike. Karate-ka can perform strikes with either hand. This book describes right-hand strikes.

Stances

Stances are the basis of every karate movement. A karate-ka learns these standing positions at the beginning of her karate training. Two common stances for strikes are the straddle-leg stance and the front stance.

Beginning karate students learn basic strikes.

Straddle-Leg Stance

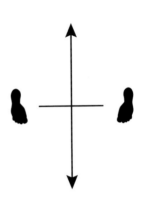

Front Stance

But a karate-ka can deliver a punch from most stances.

A karate-ka stands with her legs out to her sides in the straddle-leg stance. Her feet are two shoulder widths apart and point forward. She turns her knees slightly outward and bends them. Her knees do not bend outward past her feet.

A karate-ka begins a front stance by stepping forward with one leg. She bends her front knee and keeps her back leg straight. The knee of her front leg is directly over her front foot. Her feet are shoulder width apart. She keeps her back straight. The karate-ka can have her upper body facing forward or turned to the side.

Hand Forms and the Withdrawn Position

A karate-ka holds her hand in different ways to deliver different strikes. A karate-ka forms her hand into a fist for certain kinds of strikes. She makes a fist starting with an open hand. She folds her fingers in at the middle joint. Her fingertips touch the bottom of her fingers.

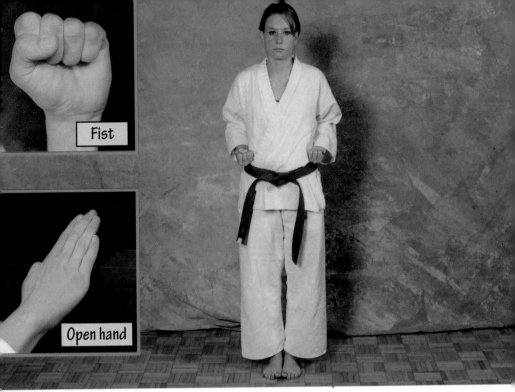

Most strikes begin with a hand in the withdrawn position.

She rolls her fingers and presses them into her palm. She then presses her thumb across her index and middle fingers.

Some karate-ka strike with their hands in open-hand positions. The karate-ka forms an open hand by holding her hand open. She presses her fingers tightly together. She bends her thumb and presses it against the side of her palm. Her wrist and the back of her hand form a straight line. She keeps her wrist tight.

Start

Finish

A karate-ka can use a back-fist strike against an opponent in front of him.

Most strikes begin with a hand in a withdrawn position. A karate-ka rests her fists on her waist slightly above her hips. The backs of her fists face the floor. She points her elbows backward.

Back-Fist Strike and Hammer-Fist Strike

Karate-ka can use back-fist strikes and hammer-fist strikes either to the side or to the front. A karate-ka begins a right side back-fist

A karate-ka swings her arm down and hits the target with the bottom of her fist during a hammer-fist strike.

strike by holding his hands in fists. His left hand is in front of his right hip. His right hand is in front of his left shoulder.

The karate-ka pulls his left hand to the withdrawn position. He moves his right elbow to his right side at the same time. His upper arm is parallel to the ground and does not extend past his side. He snaps his right forearm to the side. He strikes at the target with the knuckles of the index and middle fingers of his fist. Then he quickly withdraws his forearm.

A karate-ka begins a right, front hammer-fist strike with her hands in fists. She places her right hand near her right ear with her elbow pointing forward. She holds her left arm straight out in front of herself. She pulls her left arm to the withdrawn position. The karate-ka swings her right elbow down at the same time. Then she snaps her forearm and hits the target with the bottom of her fist. She quickly withdraws her forearm after she strikes.

Knife-hand Strike

Karate-ka aim knife-hand strikes at their opponents' upper bodies or necks. A karate-ka uses an open-hand position to perform a knife-hand strike. He strikes with the outer edge of his palm. A karate-ka can use a knife-hand strike from the inside outward. Or he can use a knife-hand strike from the outside inward.

A karate-ka begins an inside knife-hand strike with his hands in the open-hand position. He holds his right hand by his left ear with his palm facing his ear. He swings his right arm toward a target. He twists his wrist so his palm faces the floor. He then snaps his forearm at the elbow to hit the target.

He quickly withdraws his forearm after striking. He pulls his left hand into the withdrawn position as he swings his right arm toward the target. He also rotates his upper body to the left.

A karate-ka begins an outside knife-hand strike by placing his right hand by his right ear. His elbow points to the side. His upper body faces to the right. He rotates his elbow and shoulder forward and snaps his forearm toward the target. He twists his wrist at the same time so the back of his hand faces the ground. The karate-ka then withdraws his forearm.

A karate-ka begins a knife-hand strike with his hands in the open-hand position.

Chapter 4

Advanced Strikes

Skilled karate-ka learn ridge-hand strikes and palm-heel strikes. These strikes are advanced movements. Skilled karate-ka also learn to use their elbows to strike. These strikes are called elbow smashes.

Ridge-Hand Strike
The ridge-hand strike is an effective strike for attacks to an opponent's neck or groin. A karate-ka must know how to form a ridge-hand before beginning this strike. A karate-ka forms a ridge-hand by holding his hand open. He keeps his fingers straight and pressed together. He pulls his thumb to his palm. The back of his hand and his wrist are in a straight line.

Skilled karate-ka learn to use their elbows for defense.

Start

Finish

Most karate-ka use a ridge-hand strike to attack an opponent's neck.

A karate-ka begins a right ridge-hand strike by placing her right hand in the ridge-hand position. Her hand is at her waist with the palm facing upward. She pushes her right hand forward in an outward sweeping motion. She rotates her arm inward and hits her opponent's neck with the thumb-edge of her hand. The karate-ka's palm faces the floor.

Start

Finish

Some karate-ka use a palm-heel strike to hit an opponent's face or chest.

Palm-Heel Strike

Karate-ka use the palm-heel strike to hit opponents' faces or chests. A karate-ka starts with an open hand to form a palm heel. He keeps his fingers pressed together and curls them forward. His fingertips touch the bottom of his fingers. The karate-ka presses his thumb to the side of his palm. His wrist is bent back.

Start

Finish

A karate-ka can aim an elbow smash forward.

The karate-ka begins a right palm-heel strike with his left arm straight in front of him. His right hand is in the withdrawn position. He pushes his right hand forward and changes his hand to the palm-heel position. He rotates his wrist so his palm is facing forward. The karate-ka uses the bottom of his palm to hit the target. He returns his right hand to the withdrawn position after he strikes.

Start

Finish

A karate-ka also can aim an elbow smash downward.

Elbow Smashes

A karate-ka can aim an elbow smash in many different directions. She can aim an elbow smash forward, backward, upward, or downward. She also can direct an elbow smash to her left side or right side.

A karate-ka begins a right forward elbow smash with both hands in the withdrawn position. She pushes her elbow forward. Her

fist moves to her left shoulder at the same time. She hits the target with her elbow.

A backward elbow smash is the opposite of the forward elbow smash. It begins with the arm pointing forward. The karate-ka moves her elbow to the back. She aims at a target behind her.

A karate-ka begins a right upward smash with her left hand in front of her body. She holds her left hand straight out in front of her body. Her right hand is in the withdrawn position. She pulls her left fist to the withdrawn position. She pushes her right elbow forward and upward at the same time. The movement ends with her right fist by her right ear.

A side elbow smash begins with a karate-ka's hand in the withdrawn position. He places his right fist near the front of his left shoulder. The back of his fist faces the floor. He moves his left hand to the withdrawn position. The karate-ka thrusts his right elbow outward toward his right side. He turns his right wrist inward at the same time.

A karate-ka thrusts his elbow out to the side during a side elbow smash.

Chapter 5

Safety and Training

There are two main styles of karate. There are low-contact styles and high-contact styles. Shotokan karate is a low-contact style. Practice at low-contact schools involves light contact or no contact. Karate-ka at high-contact schools practice full contact during training. Karate-ka risk more injuries at high-contact schools than at low-contact schools.

All schools have rules to keep students safe. Sensei have rules about grooming, warming up, conditioning, and controlling movements. They also make sure karate-ka wear protective gear.

Karate students must learn to show respect for themselves and other people as part of their

Most sensei have rules about controlling movements.

training. Karate-ka bow to their instructor before and after class. They also bow to their partners before and after a sparring match. Sparring means to practice fighting.

Grooming

To groom means to take care of appearance and clothing. Karate-ka need to keep their bodies and uniforms clean. This is important because sweat and dirt can cause or spread illness. Karate-ka come to class clean and shower after practice.

Karate-ka must keep their fingernails and toenails trimmed. Long nails can scratch people. Karate-ka also tie back long hair for practice. They might not see a kick or a strike if they have hair in their faces.

Karate-ka remove their watches and jewelry before they practice. Jewelry could hurt the karate-ka or others. For example, a kick could tear an earring from an ear. A watch or ring could scratch another student.

Karate-ka bow to their instructor before and after class.

Warming Up and Conditioning

Karate-ka warm up before they practice. They warm up and stretch to help prevent injuries. A karate-ka might pull a muscle if he does not warm up before practicing movements.

Karate-ka exercise daily to condition their bodies. Karate-ka condition themselves by lifting weights and jogging. Exercise

strengthens their hearts, muscles, and lungs. Karate-ka who are fit are less likely to hurt themselves. They can practice karate longer without becoming tired. Tired karate-ka can become careless. Careless karate-ka might do movements wrong and hurt themselves. Or they might lose control of a movement and accidentally hurt someone else.

Sparring
Many karate-ka train so they can spar. Two karate-ka compete in a sparring match. The person who scores the most points wins. Karate-ka who compete must follow rules for sparring. These rules are meant to keep people safe.

Some karate-ka prefer no-contact or light-contact sparring. They try to stop their strikes about one inch (2.5 centimeters) from their opponents. Karate-ka who prefer high-contact sparring hit their opponents. These students still need to control their movements. Karate-ka may not hit their opponents in their

Many karate-ka train so they can spar.

faces. They learn to aim for body areas protected with pads.

Karate-ka learn to control their movements as part of their training. They control their movements so they do not hurt themselves or other students. They might twist their arms or legs the wrong way if they do a movement improperly. Or they might not know where they are swinging their legs or arms and accidentally hit another person.

Protective Gear

Tournament officials require karate-ka to wear protective gear for sparring. Karate-ka wear mouth guards and padded gloves when they compete in no-contact or light-contact sparring matches. A mouth guard protects the teeth. A kick or punch to the mouth could break or knock out unprotected teeth. Padded gloves cover the hands up to the knuckles. The gloves protect the hands for blocks or punches. Gloves also soften accidental blows to opponents.

Tournament officials require competitors to wear protective gear while sparring.

Karate-ka who prefer high-contact sparring need additional protective gear. They may wear helmets, chest protectors, forearm guards, shin guards, and foot gloves. This padded gear protects the body from hits.

Karate is an exciting sport to learn. But it can be dangerous if people do not follow the rules. It can also be dangerous if people do not wear the right protective gear. Beginning students should not try to perform advanced movements before they master basic movements. Advanced students should continue to practice basic movements. Practice and patience will help a karate-ka learn karate skills safely.

Practice and patience will help a karate-ka learn karate skills safely.

Words to Know

competition (kom-puh-TISH-uhn)—a contest of skill
condition (kuhn-DISH-uhn)—to exercise daily to keep the body fit
dojo (DOH-joh)—a karate school
gi (GEE)—a loose-fitting, cotton uniform
groom (GROOM)—to take care of appearance and clothing
injury (IN-juh-ree)—harm to the body
martial art (MAR-shuhl ART)—a style of self-defense and fighting that comes from Asia
opponent (uh-POH-nuhnt)—someone against whom a karate-ka is fighting
rotation (roh-TAY-shuhn)—a circular motion made by a body part
self-defense (SELF-di-FENSS)—the act of protecting oneself
spar (SPAHR)—to practice fighting

To Learn More

Corrigan, Ralph. *Karate Made Easy.* New York: Sterling Publications, 1995.

Gutman, Bill. *Karate.* Minneapolis: Capstone Press, 1995.

Leder, Jane Mersky. *Karate.* Learning How. Marco, Fla.: Bancroft-Sage Publishing, 1992.

Queen, J. Allen. *Start Karate!* New York: Sterling Publications, 1997.

Sieh, Ron. *Martial Arts for Beginners.* New York: Writers and Readers, 1995.

Useful Addresses

Canadian Shotokan Karate Association
1646 McPherson Drive
Port Coquitlam, BC V3C 6C9
Canada

International Society of
  Okinawan/Japanese Karate-Do
21512 Sherman Way
Canoga Park, CA 91303

Shotokan Karate of America
2500 South La Cienega Boulevard
Los Angeles, CA 90034

World Federation Karate Organization
9506 Las Tunas Drive
Temple City, CA 91780

Internet Sites

Canadian Shotokan Karate Association
http://www.geocities.com/colosseum/field/
   7270

Martial Arts Resource Page
http://www.middlebury.edu/~jswan/
   martial.arts/ma.html

Shotokan Karate for Everyone
http://members.aol.com/edl12/shotokan/
   index.htm

Shotokan Karate of America
http://www.ska.org/

Index

arm rotation, 11-12

body stretch, 11-12, 15

dojo, 7, 9

elbow smash, 27, 31, 33

Funakoshi, Gichin, 6-7

gi, 11
gloves, 40

hammer-fist strike, 17, 21-23

knife-hand strike, 17, 23, 24

mouth guard, 40

neck rotation, 11-12

Okinawa Island, 5-7
open hand, 9, 19, 20, 29
opponent, 23, 27, 28, 29, 39, 40

palm-heel strike, 27, 29-30

ridge-hand strike, 27-28

self-defense, 5, 7
sensei, 7, 35
sparring, 36, 39-40, 42
stance, 17, 19

upper body rotation, 11, 12, 15